To:

From:

Date:

with Love
INSPIRATIONAL GIFTS